Corrective Reading

Workbook

Thinking SRA Basics

Comprehension A Fast Cycle

Siegfried Engelmann
Phyllis Haddox
Susan Hanner

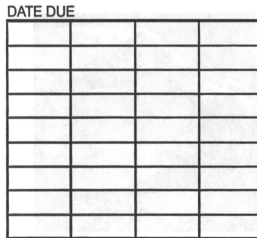

 McGraw Hill **SRA**

Columbus, OH

SRAonline.com

Send all inquiries to this address:
SRA/McGraw-Hill
4400 Easton Commons
Columbus, OH 43219

ISBN: 978-0-07-611161-9
MHID: 0-07-611161-X

2 3 4 5 6 7 8 9 QPD 13 12 11 10 09 08 07

ERRORS	1	2	3	4	TOTAL

A MAKING UP STATEMENTS

B SOME, ALL, NONE

C SAME/DIFFERENT

① ② ③ ④

D DEDUCTIONS

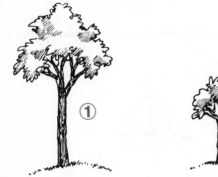 ①

 ②

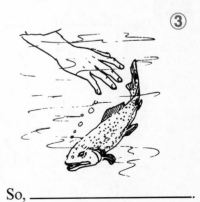 ③

All _____.

A trout _____.

So, _____.

E   MAKING UP STATEMENTS

F   DEDUCTIONS

① ② ③ ④ ⑤

G   SAME/DIFFERENT

① ② ③ ④ ⑤

H   DEDUCTIONS

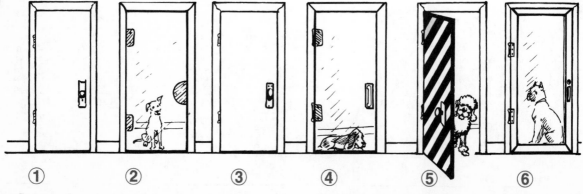

① ② ③ ④ ⑤ ⑥

A DESCRIPTION

B SOME, ALL, NONE Circle **true** or **false** for each statement you hear.

1. true false	**2.** true false	**3.** true false	**4.** true false

C SOME, ALL, NONE Underline **true** or **false** for each statement you hear.

1. true false	**2.** true false	**3.** true false	**4.** true false

D CLASSIFICATION

Underline the containers.
Circle the animals.

Lesson 2 **3**

Lesson 3

A SAME

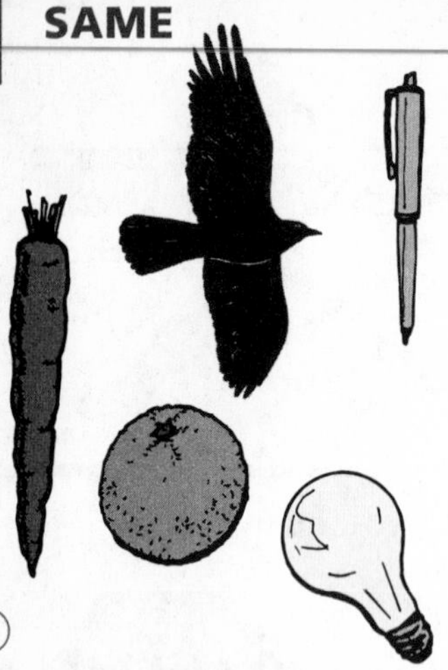

① 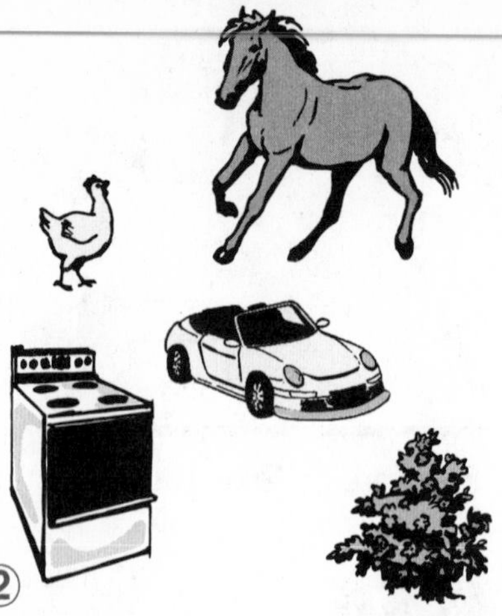 ② 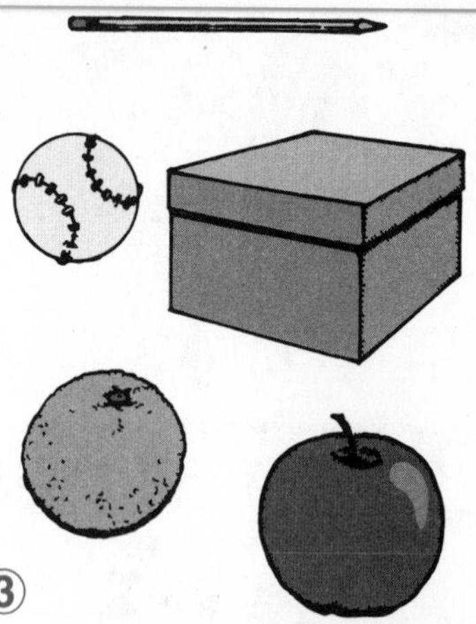 ③

B DESCRIPTION

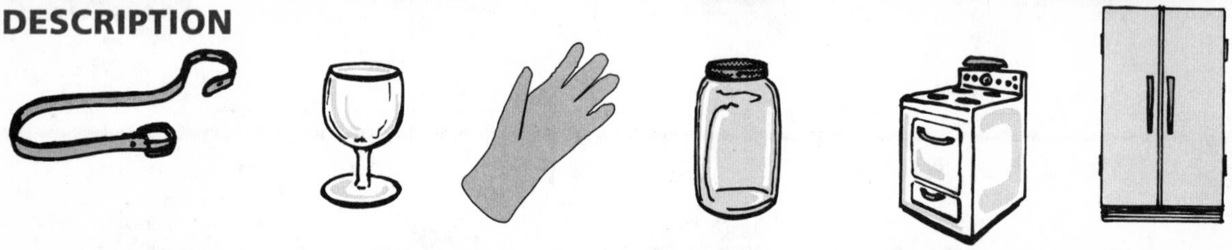

C SOME, ALL, NONE Make a box around **true** or **false** for each statement you hear.

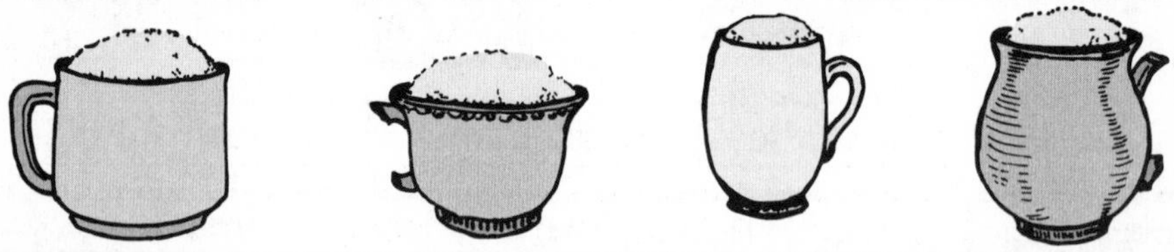

| **1.** true false | **2.** true false | **3.** true false | **4.** true false | **5.** true false |

D CLASSIFICATION

Circle the foods.
Underline the buildings.

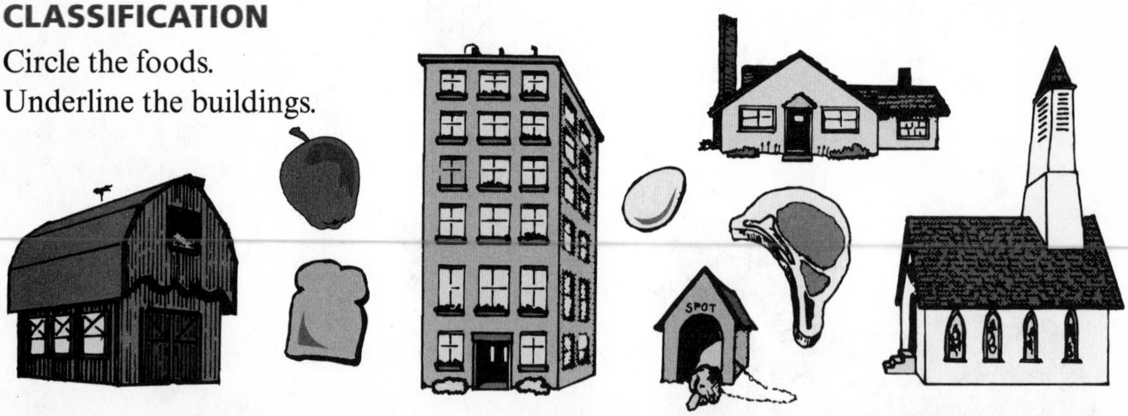

SPOT

E SOME, ALL, NONE

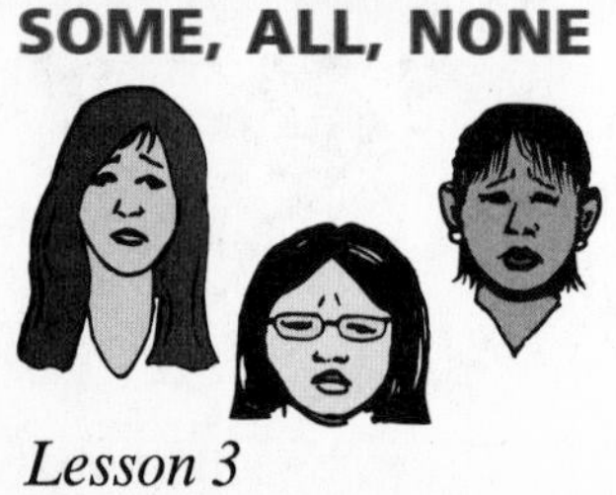

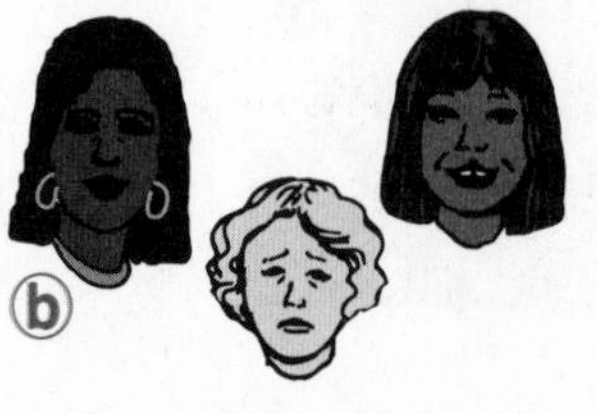

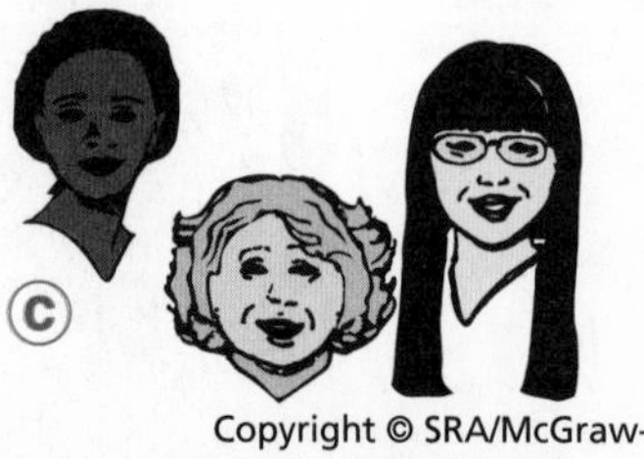

ⓐ ⓑ ⓒ

1._____
2._____
3._____

ERRORS

	1	2	3	4	TOTAL

A SAME

① ② ③

B SOME, ALL, NONE

Circle **true** or **false** for each item.

1. true false	**2.** true false	**3.** true false	**4.** true false

C CLASSIFICATION

Underline the containers. Circle the appliances.

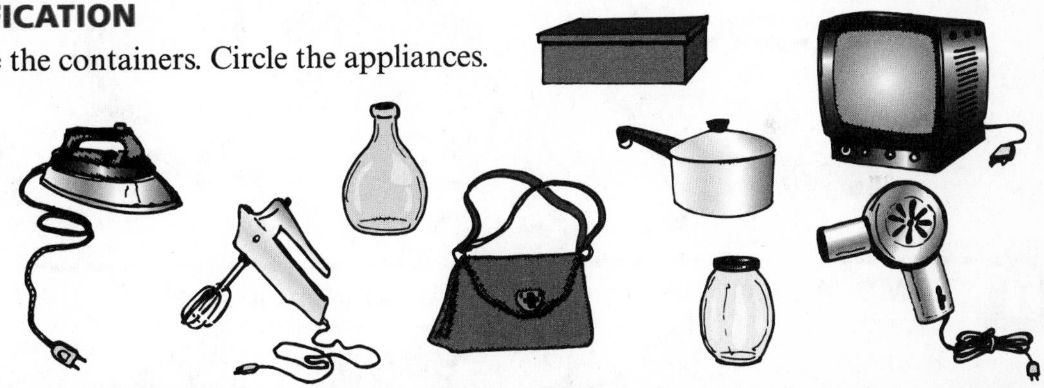

D SOME, ALL, NONE

1. _____
2. _____
3. _____

ⓐ ⓑ ⓒ

E DESCRIPTION

ERRORS | 1 | 2 | 3 | 4 | TOTAL

A DESCRIPTION

1. _____
2. _____
3. _____

B SOME, ALL, NONE

1. _____
2. _____
3. _____

C CLASSIFICATION

Circle the tools.
Underline the animals.

D SOME, ALL, NONE   Underline **true** or **false** for each item.

| **1.** true   false | **2.** true   false | **3.** true   false | **4.** true   false |

E SAME

FACT GAME SCORECARD

1	2	3	4	5	6	7	8	9	10	11	12	13	14	15
16	17	18	19	20	21	22	23	24	25	26	27	28	29	30

1	2	TOTAL

Fact Game

1

(AFTER LESSON 5)

2. All cats have teeth. Butch is a cat.

So, _____.

3. What does **masticate** mean?

4. Name the class these objects are in: bag, bottle, box, cap, purse.

5. How are a slow boat and a slow horse the same?

6. What do we call the class of animals that have a backbone and hair?

7. Name the class these objects are in: house, factory, church, store.

8. Say the first three months in a year.

9. What does **complete** mean?

10. How are a bike, a motorcycle, and a boat the same?

11. All tools help do a job. A hammer is a tool.

So, _____.

12. What's a synonym for **obtain?**

Lesson 6

ERRORS		1	2	3	4	TOTAL

A SAME

①  ② ③

B CLASSIFICATION

Make a box around the buildings.
Circle the furniture.

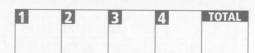

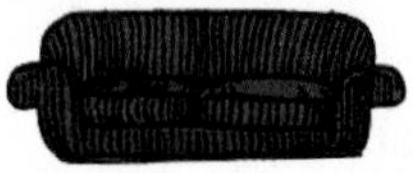

C SOME, ALL, NONE   Circle **true** or **false** for each item.

1. true false	**2.** true false	**3.** true false	**4.** true false	**5.** true false

D DESCRIPTION

ⓐ ⓑ ⓒ ⓓ

1. _____
2. _____
3. _____

8   *Lesson 6*

ERRORS | 1 | 2 | 3 | 4 | TOTAL

A SOME, ALL, NONE Circle the correct answer.

1.	true	false	maybe
2.	true	false	maybe
3.	true	false	maybe
4.	true	false	maybe
5.	true	false	maybe

B DESCRIPTION

C SAME

① ② ③

D CLASSIFICATION

Circle the foods.
Make a box around the buildings.

ERRORS

1	2	3	4	TOTAL

A SOME, ALL, NONE

Make a box around the correct answer.

1. true	false	maybe
2. true	false	maybe
3. true	false	maybe
4. true	false	maybe

B CLASSIFICATION

Underline the furniture.
Make a box around the containers.

C SAME

① ② ③

D SOME, ALL, NONE

ⓒ ⓓ ⓔ

1. _____
2. _____
3. _____
4. _____

E DESCRIPTION

ⓐ ⓑ ⓒ ⓓ

1. _____
2. _____
3. _____

A CLASSIFICATION

Make a box around the plants
Underline the foods.

B SOME, ALL, NONE

Underline the correct answer.

1. true	false	maybe	
2. true	false	maybe	
3. true	false	maybe	
4. true	false	maybe	
5. true	false	maybe	

C DESCRIPTION

ⓐ   ⓑ   ⓒ   ⓓ

1. _____
2. _____
3. _____

D SAME

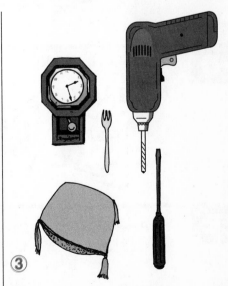

①   ②   ③

A   DESCRIPTION

B   SOME, ALL, NONE

ⓐ   ⓑ   ⓒ

1. _____
2. _____
3. _____
4. _____

C   SAME

①

②

③

D   SOME, ALL, NONE

1. true	false	maybe
2. true	false	maybe
3. true	false	maybe
4. true	false	maybe

E   1. Pass   Fail   2. Pass   Fail

F   1. Pass   Fail   2. Pass   Fail

A DESCRIPTION

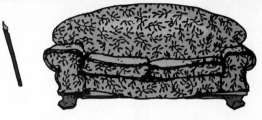

B SOME, ALL, NONE Underline the correct answer.

1. true	false	maybe
2. true	false	maybe
3. true	false	maybe
4. true	false	maybe

C SAME

①   ②   ③

Copyright © SRA/McGraw-Hill. All rights reserved.

D **CLASSIFICATION**

Circle the appliances.
Make a box around the vehicles.

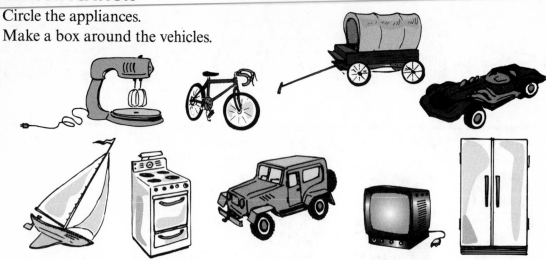

ERRORS	1	2	3	4	TOTAL

A TRUE—FALSE

1. true	false	maybe
2. true	false	maybe
3. true	false	maybe
4. true	false	maybe

B DESCRIPTION

C SOME, ALL, NONE

  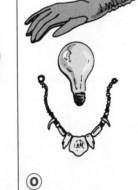

1. _____
2. _____
3. _____
4. _____

ⓜ    ⓝ 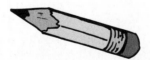   ⓞ

D SOME, ALL, NONE

1. true false	**2.** true false	**3.** true false	**4.** true false	**5.** true false

ERRORS | 1 | 2 | 3 | 4 | TOTAL

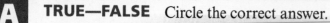

A TRUE—FALSE Circle the correct answer.

1. true   false   maybe

2. true   false   maybe

3. true   false   maybe

4. true   false   maybe

B DESCRIPTION

ⓐ   ⓑ   ⓒ   ⓓ

1. _____

2. _____

3. _____

C DESCRIPTION

D TRUE—FALSE
Circle the correct answer.

1. true   false   maybe

2. true   false   maybe

3. true   false   maybe

4. true   false   maybe

5. true   false   maybe

6. true   false   maybe

1	2	3	4	TOTAL

A DESCRIPTION

B TRUE—FALSE Underline the correct answer.

1.	true	false	maybe
2.	true	false	maybe
3.	true	false	maybe
4.	true	false	maybe
5.	true	false	maybe
6.	true	false	maybe

C TRUE—FALSE Make a box around the correct answer.

1.	true	false	maybe	5.	true	false	maybe
2.	true	false	maybe	6.	true	false	maybe
3.	true	false	maybe	7.	true	false	maybe
4.	true	false	maybe				

D SOME, ALL, NONE

1. _____
2. _____
3. _____
4. _____

ⓐ   ⓑ   ⓒ

ERRORS		1	2	3	4	TOTAL

A **TRUE—FALSE** Circle the correct answer.

1. true false maybe

2. true false maybe

3. true false maybe

4. true false maybe

5. true false maybe

6. true false maybe

B **DESCRIPTION**

C **TRUE—FALSE** Circle the correct answer.

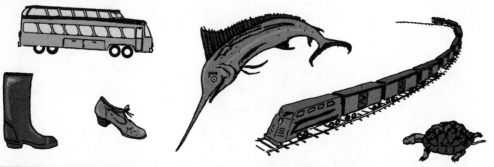

1. true false maybe

2. true false maybe

3. true false maybe

4. true false maybe

5. true false maybe

6. true false maybe

D **DESCRIPTION**

ⓐ ⓑ ⓒ ⓓ

1. _____

2. _____

3. _____

18 *Lesson 15*

FACT GAME SCORECARD

1	2	3	4	5	6	7	8	9	10	11	12	13	14	15
16	17	18	19	20	21	22	23	24	25	26	27	28	29	30

1	**2**	**TOTAL**

Fact Game

2

(AFTER LESSON 15)

2. What's a synonym for **leap?**

3. All fish have gills. A trout is a fish.
What does the rule let you know about a trout?

4. What does an astronomer do?

5. Name three classes of animals that have a backbone.

6. What does **descend** mean?

7. Say the 2 facts you've learned about all birds.

8. Some felines have stripes. A cougar is a feline.
So, ——————————————————.

9. Name the months of the year.

10. What does **amble** mean?

11. Every animal eats. A zebra is an animal.
So, ——————————————————.

12. What is an **exposition?**

ERRORS

1	2	3	4	TOTAL

A TRUE—FALSE Underline the correct answer.

1.	true	false	maybe
2.	true	false	maybe
3.	true	false	maybe
4.	true	false	maybe
5.	true	false	maybe
6.	true	false	maybe
7.	true	false	maybe

B SOME, ALL, NONE

ⓐ ⓑ ⓒ

1. _____
2. _____
3. _____
4. _____

C-1 ANALOGIES

is to

AS

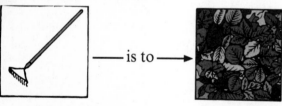

is to

C-2 ANALOGIES

 is to

AS

is to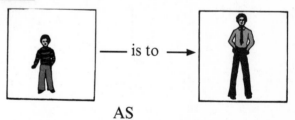

D DESCRIPTION Write the letter of the fish described.

ⓐ ⓑ ⓒ ⓓ

1. _____
2. _____
3. _____

E CLASSIFICATION

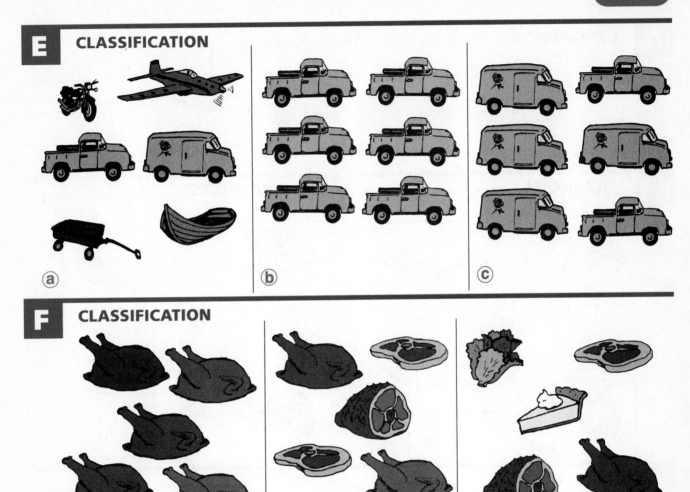

ⓐ ⓑ ⓒ

F CLASSIFICATION

ⓐ ⓑ ⓒ

ERRORS | 1 | 2 | 3 | 4 | TOTAL

A DESCRIPTION   Write the letter of the cake described.

ⓐ   ⓑ   ⓒ   ⓓ

1. _____

2. _____

3. _____

B-1 ANALOGIES

is to →

AS

is to →

B-2 ANALOGIES

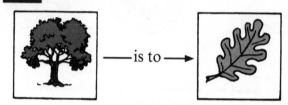

is to →

AS

is to →

C TRUE—FALSE   Circle the correct answer.

1. true	false	maybe
2. true	false	maybe
3. true	false	maybe
4. true	false	maybe
5. true	false	maybe
6. true	false	maybe

D CLASSIFICATION

ⓐ

ⓑ

ⓒ

A   DEDUCTIONS   Write **true**, **false**, or **maybe**.

Here's the only thing Fred did. Fred shined the long shoes.

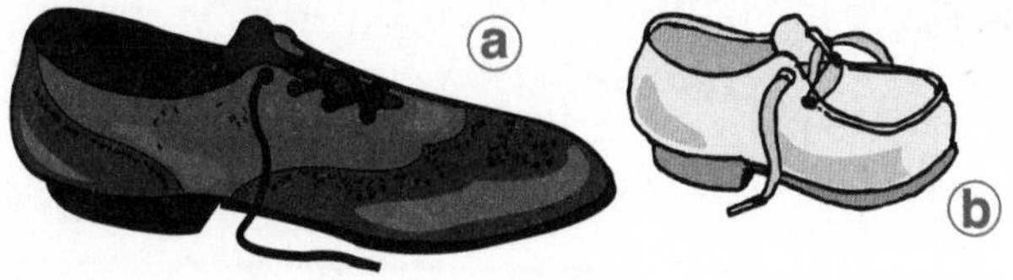

1. Fred shined object B. _____

2. Fred shined object C. _____

3. Fred did not shine object D. _____

B   INDUCTIONS   Figure out the rule for the triangles. Then draw two more triangles.

①   ②   ③   ④   ⑤

C   ANALOGIES   Complete the analogy by circling the correct picture.

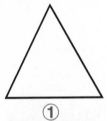

is to

AS

is to

D   CLASSIFICATION

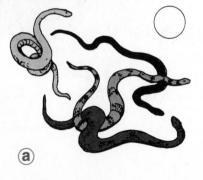
ⓐ
_____

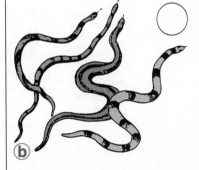
ⓑ

ⓒ

reptiles   striped snakes   snakes

ERRORS

1	2	3	4	TOTAL

A INDUCTIONS   Figure out the rule for the lines. Then draw more lines.

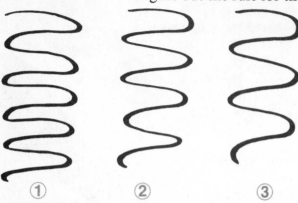

①   ②   ③   ④   ⑤

B DEDUCTIONS   Write **true**, **false**, or **maybe**.

> **Here's the only thing the woman did.**
> **The woman wore some of the tall hats.**

ⓐ   ⓑ   ⓒ   ⓓ

1. The woman wore object A.   _____

2. The woman wore object D.   _____

3. The woman did not wear object D.   _____

C DEDUCTIONS   Write **true**, **false**, or **maybe**.

> **Here's the only thing the fire did. The fire burned fat logs.**

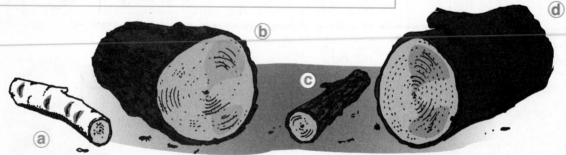

1. The fire burned object A.   _____

2. The fire did not burn object B.   _____

3. The fire burned object C.   _____

D CLASSIFICATION

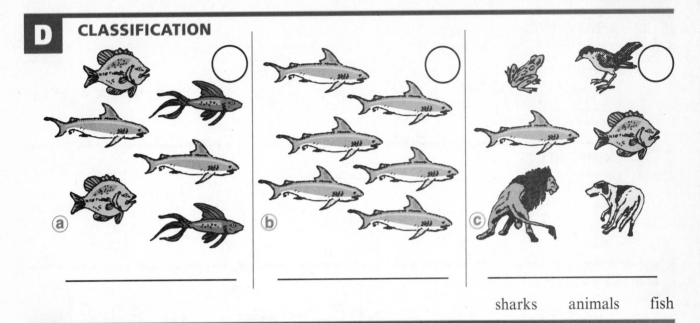

sharks   animals   fish

E ANALOGIES   Complete the analogy by circling the correct picture.

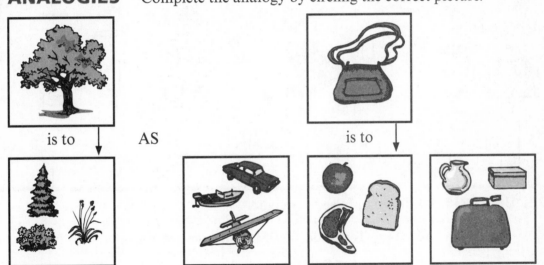

is to   AS   is to

Lesson 20

ERRORS

TOTAL

TEST 2

A ANALOGIES

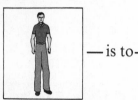

 — is to → AS is to →

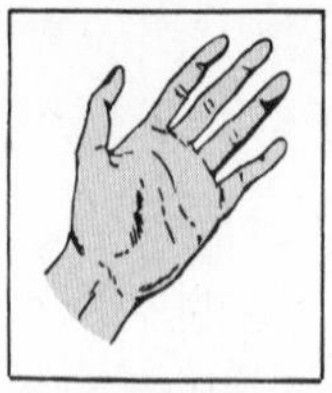

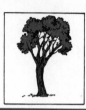

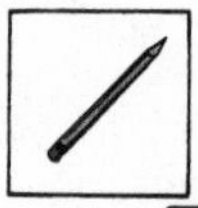

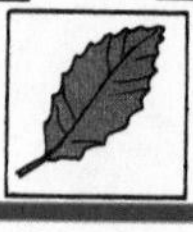

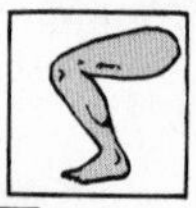

B INDUCTIONS

① ② ③ ④ ⑤

C CLASSIFICATION

ⓐ

ⓑ

ⓒ

_______________ _______________ _______________

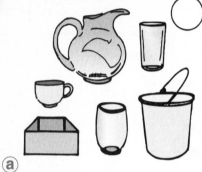

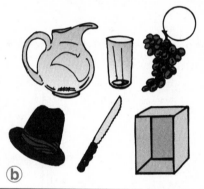

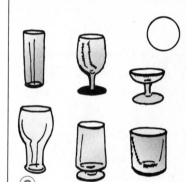

containers objects glasses

D DEDUCTIONS Write **true, false,** or **maybe.**

Here's the only thing Terry did. Terry made some of the small bowls.

ⓐ

ⓑ

ⓒ

ⓓ

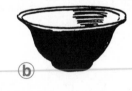

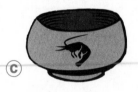

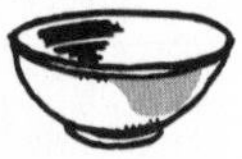

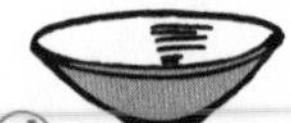

1. Terry made object D. _______________

2. Terry made object B. _______________

3. Terry did not make object C. _______________

E

1. Pass Fail

F

1. Pass Fail **3.** Pass Fail

2. Pass Fail

ERRORS | | 1 | 2 | 3 | 4 | TOTAL

A DEDUCTIONS Write **true**, **false**, or **maybe**.

> Here's the only thing we know about Fred. Fred did not drive the long cars.

ⓐ　　　　ⓑ　　　　ⓒ

1. Fred drove object C. _____

2. Fred drove object B. _____

3. Fred drove object A. _____

B INDUCTIONS Figure out the rule for the triangles. Then draw triangles 2 and 5.

① 　　② 　　③ 　　④ 　　⑤

C ANALOGIES Complete the analogy.

A bird is to flying as a fish is to _____.

walking
swimming
talking

D CLASSIFICATION

ⓐ

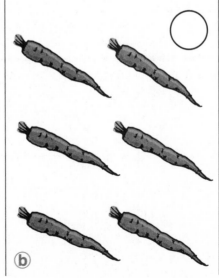

ⓑ

ⓒ

_____　　_____

living things　　carrots　　plants

Lesson 22

ERRORS		1	2	3	4	TOTAL

A CLASSIFICATION

①   ②   ③   ④

____   ____   ____   ____

____   ____   ____   ____

____   ____   ____   ____

B DEDUCTIONS   Write **true, false,** or **maybe.**

> **Here's the only thing we know about Jane.**
> **Jane did not swing the black bats.**

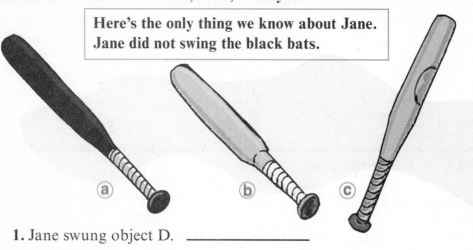

ⓐ   ⓑ   ⓒ   ⓓ

1. Jane swung object D. _____

2. Jane swung object C. _____

3. Jane swung object B. _____

C INDUCTIONS   Figure out the rule. Then draw rectangles 2 and 4.

①   ②   ③   ④   ⑤

28   *Lesson 22*

D CLASSIFICATION

ⓐ   ⓑ   ⓒ

_____   _____

shoes   objects   clothing

E ANALOGIES   Complete the analogy.

A pencil is to wood as a nail is to _____.

metal
plastic
paper

ERRORS		1	2	3	4	TOTAL

A INDUCTIONS Figure out how each row changes.

① ② ③ ④ ⑤

B CLASSIFICATION

① ② ③ ④ ⑤

P – men
Z – tall men
D – men wearing hats
L – short men
R – men wearing jackets
B – men without hats
C – men without jackets

_____ _____ _____ _____ _____

_____ _____ _____ _____ _____

_____ _____ _____ _____ _____

_____ _____ _____ _____ _____

C ANALOGIES

A hammer is to tools as meat is to _____.

food
red
soft

D DESCRIPTION

ⓐ ⓑ ⓒ ⓓ

1. _____

2. _____

3. _____

| 1 | 2 | 3 | 4 | TOTAL |

A CLASSIFICATION

① ② ③ ④ ⑤

E – food
I – foods that are in a pan
O – foods that are on a plate
U – foods that are round
A – fried eggs
B – foods that are long

B INDUCTIONS

① ② ③

1. While the bell was ringing, a woman brushed her hair.
2. While the bell was ringing, a woman read a book.
3. While the bell was ringing, a woman bent over.

C INDUCTIONS   Figure how each row changes.

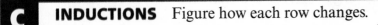

① ② ③ ④ ⑤

D DESCRIPTION

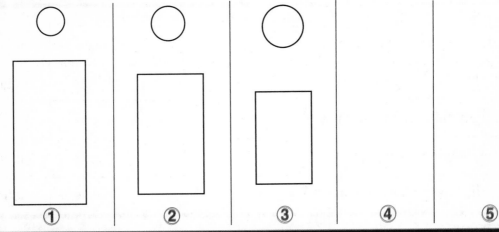

ⓐ ⓑ ⓒ ⓓ

1. _____
2. _____
3. _____

ERRORS

1	2	3	4	TOTAL

A CLASSIFICATION

① ② ③ ④ ⑤

___ ___ ___ ___ ___

___ ___ ___ ___ ___

___ ___ ___ ___ ___

___ ___ ___

B INDUCTIONS Figure out how each row changes.

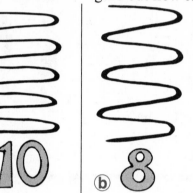

ⓐ 10 ⓑ 8 ⓒ ⓓ ⓔ 2

C SAME

1. standing on your head, slipping, snoring	objects	actions
2. shoes, truck, pants, box, pen	objects	actions
3. lighting a match, ignore, chew	objects	actions
4. yelling, singing a song, read	objects	actions
5. football, towel, glass, magazine	objects	actions

D INDUCTIONS

1. While the fire was burning, a man wore a coat.
2. While the fire was burning, a man chopped wood.
3. While the fire was burning, a man wore a hat.

FACT GAME SCORECARD

1	2	3	4	5	6	7	8	9	10	11	12	13	14	15
16	17	18	19	20	21	22	23	24	25	26	27	28	29	30

1	2	TOTAL

2. What word means **to use up** or **eat?**

3. Finish this analogy.
A **man** is to **hand** as a **feline** is to _____.

4. Tell the 2 facts about all amphibians.

5. What's a synonym for **close?**

6. What is the date of Halloween?

7. What's the opposite of **long?**

8. What's a synonym for **comprehend?**

9. What's a synonym for **duplicate?**

10. What's the opposite of **shallow?**

11. Driving a car. Object or action?

12. What's the opposite of **narrow?**

ERRORS | 1 | 2 | 3 | 4 | TOTAL

A INDUCTIONS

1. When the moon was half full, a tiger roared.
2. When the moon was half full, a tiger chased a butterfly.
3. When the moon was half full, a tiger drank from a river.

B CLASSIFICATION

ⓐ   ⓑ   ⓒ

_____   _____   _____

human beings   women   mammals

C ANALOGIES

A pen is to writing as a knife is to _____.

blade
handle
cutting

D SAME

	objects	actions
1. reading, wearing a coat, descend, go	objects	actions
2. drinking coffee, pull, fall, seeing	objects	actions
3. coffee, bus, coats, airplane, sharks	objects	actions
4. talking, duplicate, sipping a milkshake	objects	actions
5. popcorn, milkshake, notebook, canine	objects	actions

E INDUCTIONS Figure out how each row changes.

ERRORS | 1 | 2 | 3 | 4 | TOTAL

A DEDUCTIONS Write **true, false,** or **maybe.**

> Here's the only thing Sue did.
> Sue wore some of the white shirts.

ⓐ ⓑ ⓒ ⓓ ⓔ

1. Sue wore object A. _____

2. Sue did not wear object C. _____

3. Sue wore object D. _____

B SAME

1. motorcycle, ink, lamp	objects	actions	tell what kind
2. hot, sticky, lumpy	objects	actions	tell what kind
3. skates, water, picture	objects	actions	tell what kind
4. mean, happy, quick	objects	actions	tell what kind
5. envelope, flower, shell	objects	actions	tell what kind

C ANALOGIES

Christmas is to December as Independence Day is to _____.

June
January
July

D DESCRIPTION Write the letter of the object when it is described.

ⓐ ⓑ ⓒ ⓓ

1. _____

2. _____

3. _____

ERRORS

	1	2	3	4	TOTAL

A CLASSIFICATION

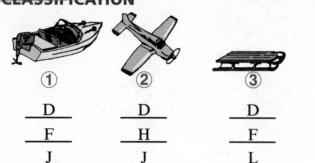

①   ②   ③   ④   ⑤

①	②	③	④	⑤
D	D	D	D	D
F	H	F	H	H
J	J	L	L	J
M	M	O	O	O

B ANALOGIES

People are to skin as trees are to _____.   bark   skin   green

C DEDUCTIONS   Write **true**, **false**, or **maybe**.

> Here's the only thing Cleo will do.
> Cleo will wash none of the dirty plates.

      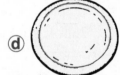

ⓐ   ⓑ   ⓒ   ⓓ

1. Cleo will wash object B.   _____

2. Cleo will wash object D.   _____

3. Cleo will wash object A.   _____

D SAME

1. dirty, broken, clean	objects	actions	tell what kind
2. clouds, man, mountain	objects	actions	tell what kind
3. flying, sweep, pour	objects	actions	tell what kind
4. hit, fishing, weep	objects	actions	tell what kind
5. leaves, pins, card	objects	actions	tell what kind

E CLASSIFICATION

Make a box around the herbivorous animals.
Circle the carnivorous animals.

ERRORS | 1 | 2 | 3 | 4 | TOTAL

A CLASSIFICATION

①   ②   ③   ④

___   ___   ___   ___

___   ___   ___   ___

___   ___   ___   ___

B ANALOGIES

A leopard is to spots as a zebra is to _____ .

stripes
dots
checks

C SAME

1. vehicles, appliance, animal	objects	actions	tell what kind
2. pitcher, stove, bread	objects	actions	tell what kind
3. climb, shout, spell	objects	actions	tell what kind
4. thin, purple, plastic	objects	actions	tell what kind
5. real, hard, soft	objects	actions	tell what kind

D DEDUCTIONS   Write **true, false,** or **maybe.**

Here's the only thing Dan did. Dan chased some white ducks.

ⓐ   ⓑ   ⓒ   ⓓ

1. Dan chased object C.   _____

2. Dan did not chase object B.   _____

3. Dan chased object A.   _____

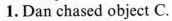

A SAME

1. shiny, long, fat	objects	actions	tell what kind
2. flower, canine, bike	objects	actions	tell what kind
3. blanket, street, purse	objects	actions	tell what kind
4. modify, run, sew	objects	actions	tell what kind
5. dull, insolent, striped	objects	actions	tell what kind

B CLASSIFICATION

Underline the carnivorous animals.
Circle the herbivorous animals.

C DESCRIPTION

(a)   (b)   (c)   (d)

1. _____
2. _____
3. _____

D CLASSIFICATION

①   ②   ③   ④   ⑤

R	R	R	R	R
T	X	T	T	X
M	A	M	A	M
C	B	B	C	C

1. Pass   Fail   **2.** Pass   Fail   **3.** Pass   Fail

A DESCRIPTION

B DESCRIPTION

C SOME, ALL, NONE

1. _____
2. _____
3. _____

ⓐ   ⓑ   ⓒ

D SOME, ALL, NONE

1. _____
2. _____
3. _____
4. _____

ⓒ   ⓓ   ⓔ

E SAME

Review for Test 1   **39**

F SAME

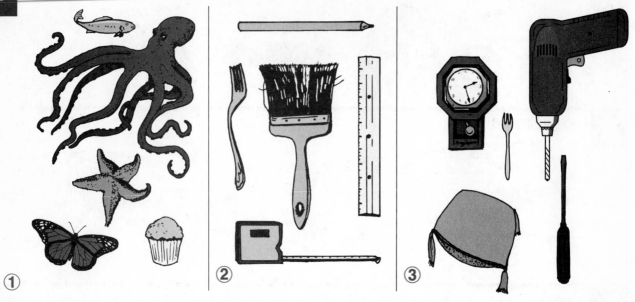

① ② ③

G SOME, ALL, NONE
Make a box around the correct answer.

1. true	false	maybe
2. true	false	maybe
3. true	false	maybe
4. true	false	maybe

H SOME, ALL, NONE Underline the correct answer.

1. true	false	maybe
2. true	false	maybe
3. true	false	maybe
4. true	false	maybe
5. true	false	maybe

A-1 ANALOGIES

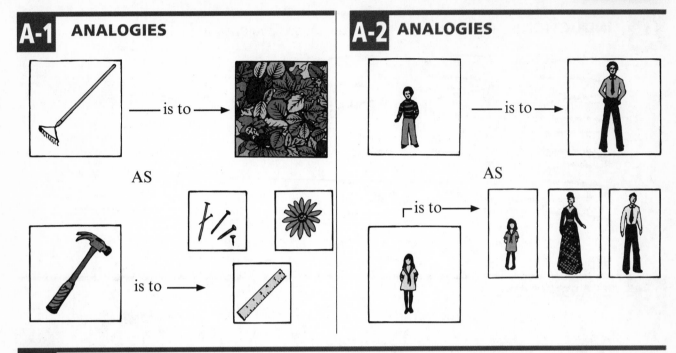

A-2 ANALOGIES

B ANALOGIES Complete the analogy by circling the correct picture.

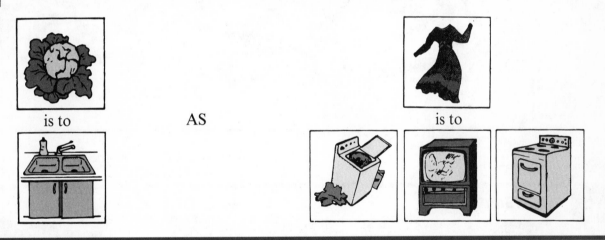

is to   AS   is to

C INDUCTIONS Figure out the rule for the triangles. Then draw two more triangles.

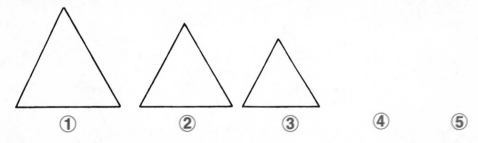

① ② ③ ④ ⑤

Review for Test 2   **41**

D **INDUCTIONS** Figure out the rule for the lines. Then draw more lines.

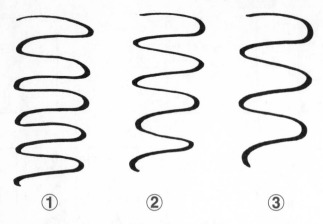

① ② ③ ④ ⑤

E **CLASSIFICATION**

 ⓐ

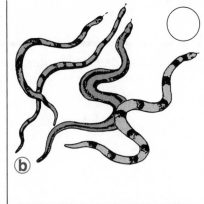 ⓑ

 ⓒ

_____ _____ _____

reptiles   striped snakes   snakes

F **CLASSIFICATION**

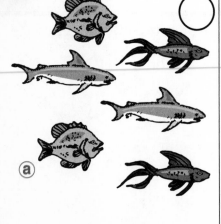 ⓐ

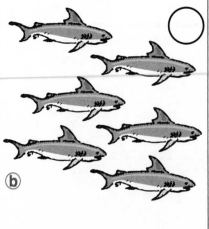 ⓑ

 ⓒ

_____ _____ _____

sharks   animals   fish

G DEDUCTIONS Write **true, false,** or **maybe.**

> **Here's the only thing the woman did.**
> **The woman wore some of the tall hats.**

 ⓐ  ⓑ 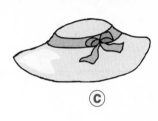 ⓒ  ⓓ

1. The woman wore object A. _____

2. The woman wore object D. _____

3. The woman did not wear object D. _____

H DEDUCTIONS Write **true, false,** or **maybe.**

> **Here's the only thing the fire did.**
> **The fire burned fat logs.**

1. The fire burned object A. _____

2. The fire did not burn object B. _____

3. The fire burned object C. _____

Test 3 Review (Lesson 30)

A SAME

1. dirty, broken, clean	objects	actions	tell what kind
2. clouds, man, mountain	objects	actions	tell what kind
3. flying, sweep, pour	objects	actions	tell what kind
4. hit, fishing, weep	objects	actions	tell what kind
5. leaves, pins, card	objects	actions	tell what kind

B SAME

1. vehicles, appliance, animal	objects	actions	tell what kind
2. pitcher, stove, bread	objects	actions	tell what kind
3. climb, shout, spell	objects	actions	tell what kind
4. thin, purple, plastic	objects	actions	tell what kind
5. real, hard, soft	objects	actions	tell what kind

C CLASSIFICATION

Make a box around the herbivorous animals.
Circle the carnivorous animals.

D **CLASSIFICATION** Circle the appliances. Make a box around the vehicles.

E **DESCRIPTION**

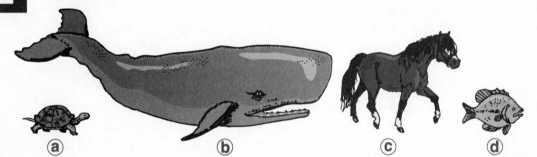

ⓐ　　　　ⓑ　　　　ⓒ　　　　ⓓ

1. _____
2. _____
3. _____

F **DESCRIPTION**

ⓐ　　　　ⓑ　　　　ⓒ　　　　ⓓ

1. _____
2. _____
3. _____

G CLASSIFICATION

①	②	③	④	⑤
D	D	D	D	D
F	H	F	H	H
J	J	L	L	J
M	M	O	O	O

H CLASSIFICATION

①	②	③	④
___	___	___	___
___	___	___	___
___	___	___	___